PELE
THE HAWAIIAN VOLCANO GODDESS

Joseph Mullins

Mutual Publishing

Oil painting by Jules Tavernier titled "The Crater of Kilauea, Island of Hawaii," dated 1885. Tavernier, a French-born English painter, spent four years in the islands in the late 1880s. While on a sketching tour of Hawai'i Island in January 1885, he witnessed the awe-inspiring eruption of Kīlauea which lead to the Volcano School, a regional movement exclusive to Hawai'i. With fellow artists Charles Furneaux and Joseph D. Strong, he captured Kīlauea's explosive, spectacular volcanic activity for the world to see. His paintings were included in the art collections of King Kalākaua and the Emperor of Japan. RUSSELL-COTES ART GALLERY & MUSEUM, DOREST, ENGLAND.

PREVIOUS PAGE: *A towering lava fountain during the eruption of Kīlauea Iki in 1959.* PHOTO BY L. PETERSON. NATIONAL PARK SERVICE

Originally published with the title *The Goddess Pele* © 1977 by Aloha Graphics and Sales

ISBN: 978-1-949307-62-7
Library of Congress Control Number available upon request.

Front cover photo © Galyna Andrushko | Dreamstime.com
Back cover photo © Robert Schlie | Dreamstime.com

Layout and design by Jane Gillespie
First Printing, June 2024

Mutual Publishing, LLC
1215 Center Street, Suite 210 | Honolulu, Hawaii 96816
Ph: 808-732-1709 | Fax: 808-734-4094
email: info@mutualpublishing.com | www.mutualpublishing.com

Printed in South Korea

Oil painting by Jules Tavernier titled "Halema'uma'u Crater, Kilauea Volcano." dated 1887. ISAACS ART CENTER

CONTENTS

The Hawaiian Religion 5

Meet Pele 8

The Legend of ʻŌhiʻa and Lehua 10

Bad Luck on The Big Island 12

Pele's Country 13

Pele's High Mountains 17

Pele and the Missionaries 20

How Pele Came to Kīlauea 22

A Priestess of Pele 24

A Chiefess Defies Pele 26

Oil painting by Jules Tavernier titled "Kilauea Caldera," circa 1885-86.

Pele—Down, But Not Out 30

The Fury of Pele 33

1924 Explosions 37

Volcano House 42

Putting Pele's Energy to Work 47

A Personal Appearance 50

Pele's Several Forms 52

You Can't (Shouldn't) Take it with You 54

Suggested Reading 55

THE HAWAIIAN RELIGION

Of all the gods of ancient Hawai‘i, only Pele, the volcano goddess, still lives in the hearts of many Hawaiian and even non-Hawaiian residents of the islands. To some, she is a powerful and very real presence, especially in the Volcano region of the Big Island. To believers, this is her present home after having resided during past ages on other islands in the Hawaiian chain. To many in Hawai‘i she is the subject of colorful legends with which to beguile wide-eyed visitors. Others cynically utilize her name to glamorize their perfumes, statuettes, or whatever other saleable object or product they can logically associate with her. To a geologist, her story is seen as the ancient Hawaiian's way of explaining the unknown natural forces that periodically devastated the land with lava flows or put on spectacular fiery displays of what must have seemed supernatural powers. But to all who live in the Hawaiian Islands—believer or cynic—Pele is an aspect of the Hawai‘i of old that is constantly alive.

A lei offering for Pele. SHINY THINGS. WWW.FLICKR.COM/WIKIMEDIACOMMONS

Pu'uhonua o Hōnaunau in South Kona on Hawai'i Island, the Place of Refuge, was the largest of ten pu'uhonua on the island. The pu'uhonua stood as sanctuaries in a society ruled by the kapu. Kapu-breakers who reached them escaped the death penalty. In times of war, women, children, and those who were not fighters could also find safety in pu'uhonua. RONPAUL86/WIKIMEDIACOMMONS

Ancient Beliefs

Kū, the god of war. WIKIMEDIACOMMONS

The peoples of ancient Polynesia were scattered on tiny island groups over an immense expanse of the world's largest ocean. Despite the vast distances separating them, Polynesians were similar in appearance wherever found. Samoans, Tahitians, Maoris or Hawaiians, they were basically one people. There were local variations in culture, but the underlying elements were the same. Even their languages were major dialects of one overall Polynesian language.

The same was true of religion. Thus, the Hawaiian religion resembled the other religions of Polynesia in its general theology. The Hawaiians recognized four great gods and a veritable host of lesser gods, ʻaumakua (family or personal god), spirits, and semi-divine heroes such as Māui. The major gods represented the universal forces of nature: Lono the god of fertility; Kāne the creator of many things; Kanaloa the sea god; and Kū the war god.

The lesser gods were usually associated with particular activities or places. Of these, the most famous is Pele, the volcano goddess, who is intimately associated with the active volcanic region on the Island of Hawaiʻi, though there are legends about Pele attached to many localities in all the Hawaiian Islands.

Members of a ceremonial procession present hoʻokupu (gifts)to the Hawaiian god Lono during the Makahiki festival at Bellows Air Force Station in Waimānalo, Oʻahu, in 2010. The Makahiki season which aligns with the rainy season from mid-November to late-January/February is a time of relaxation, games, and harvest. USMC

A slow-moving river of lava from Kīlauea. IVA VANUROVA | DREAMSTIME.COM

Meet Pele

Picture a beautiful woman given to ferocious tantrums of rage and jealousy. When aroused, she stamps her foot on the earth, causing it to tremble with earthquakes. Cracks yawn in the soil and she calls forth torrents of molten lava which race after those who have angered her. The goddess herself rides the leading wave of rushing liquid rock, screaming imprecations and throwing red hot boulders at her fleeing quarry. Anger, jealousy, bad temper—that's one side of Pele, indeed her predominant side.

Roughly the same theme runs through almost every one of the multitude of Pele legends found in ancient Hawaiian mythology. Pele bursts into righteous anger over a lost or unfaithful lover, a contest she failed to win, or a denial of something she desired. Despite her angry nature, many Pele stories recount her acts of kindness toward her people in times of famine or drought.

When Pele appeared to people in human form, she was usually seen as a beautiful young woman with golden hair. At other times, particularly along the seacoast, she took the form of an old woman.

To this day, people in the Puna and Ka'ū coastal regions of the Big Island treat an unknown old woman with considerable deference, especially if met with on a lonely road or trail.

In many of the legends, Pele is accompanied by her youngest sister Hi'iaka, whose character differs radically from that of Pele. Hi'iaka is open, friendly, generous, and helpful in contrast to the distrustful and vindictive nature of the volcano goddess. When Pele appeared as a beautiful young woman, she was seen as blonde and fair-skinned while her sister was a redhead, neither of the two being at all typical of normal Polynesian complexion and hair.

The younger sister constantly helps mortals in trouble and strives to combat injustices. Totally loyal in her service to Pele, Hi'iaka is all too often repaid with broken promises and cruel, destructive acts. In modern terms, Pele's behavior might be classed as schizophrenic, her kindly and gentle side at war with and unable to control the hot-tempered other half.

Pele had eight other sisters who, wise to her capricious ways, avoided displeasing her. They too were goddesses but none was so powerful as Pele. All were named Hi'iaka, but with a distinguishing additional name. Pele's special favorite, and the youngest, was Hi'iaka-i-ka-poli-o-Pele (Hi'iaka in the heart of Pele). It is this Hi'iaka who is referred to in most stories about Pele. Honest, trusting Hi'iaka always believed Pele's promises, a fidelity that was poorly repaid.

Pele's character can be likened to the saying, "It's not nice to fool Mother Nature." The Hawaiians of old knew well that it was dangerous to fool or defy Pele because her retribution was swift and massive. The story of 'Ōhi'a and Lehua provides an illustration of Pele's vengefulness when crossed.

'Ōhi'a lehua tree growing near Halema'uma'u crater. MIKE7777777 | DREAMSTIME.COM

The Legend of 'Ōhi'a and Lehua

There was, in the old days, a tall, handsome young chieftain named 'Ōhi'a. One day, while 'Ōhi'a was in the woods, Pele appeared to him as a lovely woman, beautifully dressed and scented. 'Ōhi'a greeted her and Pele, as was her way, could not resist bragging a bit and, the conversation having turned to surfing, she claimed that she could cause smooth seas or rough surfing waves and even tidal waves. 'Ōhi'a replied that if she could do all the things she said, then she must be a goddess.

Pele then told him that she was indeed the goddess of the volcano. She further stated, in her forthright manner, that she intended to have him for her husband. At this, 'Ōhi'a became worried because he had seen the destructive evidence of her anger along the seacoast and was aware of her volatile temperament. He had no wish to anger her, but he was in love with beautiful, young Lehua, whose sweet and gentle nature appealed to him. Still, if he refused to marry Pele and she was sincere, he would surely anger the goddess. If he said yes, and Pele was only testing his love for Lehua, her anger would be just as certain. Pele could destroy his land and kill all his people.

'Ōhi'a lehua blossoms found in Volcanoes National Park. JIM MOREFIELD. WIKIMEDIACOMMONS

In desperation and perplexity, 'Ōhi'a asked Pele to promise not to use her volcanic power no matter what his answer. She complied to his request, knowing full well she had many other powers of which the handsome young chief was unaware. 'Ōhi'a told Pele that he was under a love spell placed on him by Lehua and besides, as a mere mortal man he was unworthy of a goddess.

Pele was furious, calling him much less than a man to be so weak and susceptible to a spell. Although she had promised not to send lava over the land to destroy 'Ōhi'a's people, she had many other powers on call. In the throes of her savage fury, she changed 'Ōhi'a into a twisted and ugly tree with grayish leaves.

When Lehua heard what Pele had done to her loved one, she begged the goddess to repair the damage, even offering her own life in exchange for that of 'Ōhi'a. But Pele ignored the girl's pleas and returned sulking to her home in the fire pit of Halema'uma'u. Pele's callous cruelty even angered the other gods, but nothing they did could change 'Ōhi'a back into a man. At last they decided on a plan to unite the lovers forever. They changed Lehua into a scarlet blossom on the tree of 'ōhi'a. Thus, the young chief and his beloved are together for eternity, and to this day the blossom is called 'ōhi'a lehua.

BAD LUCK ON THE BIG ISLAND

Top: *'Ōhelo berries growing on lava within Kīlauea Iki crater.* GAVRIL MARGITTAI | DREAMSTIME.COM
Bottom: *A ho'okupu left for Pele.* KAZUNORI SANO | DREAMSTIME.COM

Many old traditions and customs associated with Pele are still practiced by residents and even visitors to the region of Kīlauea, where Pele resides in the fire pit of Halema'uma'u. The 'ōhelo berry grows only in this region and it is one of Pele's sacred plants. It is thought to be bad luck to eat the 'ōhelo berry without first offering a few to Pele by tossing them in the direction of her home.

In early 1974, a segment of the popular *Hawaii Five-O* television series was being filmed on the Big Island. During the filming crew's entire stay they were plagued by rains which delayed production. Even when they tried filming at Waimea, the normally sunny northwestern section of the island, a long standing drought was broken. Before the film crew arrived, usually rainy Hilo had enjoyed three weeks of sunshine and clear blue skies. Honolulu newspapers implied that production personnel might have incurred Pele's displeasure by inadvertent actions. It seems that some crew members had eaten 'ōhelo berries without first offering some to Pele and had gathered up souvenir pieces of lava from a recent eruption flow. Either one of these actions was enough to anger the goddess according to believers. Was *Hawaii Five-O*'s bad luck mere coincidence? Certainly many people in Hawai'i see nothing coincidental about the rains that hampered the television program's filming.

PELE'S COUNTRY

Pele, the volcano goddess, lives today in a peculiarly befitting region, a strange domain rich in natural wonders and abrupt contrasts. On one side of Kīlauea, dripping-wet rain forests of ʻōhiʻa trees and primeval giant tree ferns seem like the terrain of prehistoric times when dinosaurs walked the earth. With almost unbelievable suddenness, this humid forest verges on the other side into barren lava lands that look as if they had never seen a drop of rain. Steaming fumaroles emit clouds of vapor that drift spirit-like through the daylight's bright sunshine and sparkling clear air.

By night, the eerie silence and swirling mists are reminiscent of scenes from a Gothic novel or the movie, *The Hound of the Baskervilles*. During eruptions, the dusky stillness is shattered by the rumble and hiss of lava pouring from deep within the earth. Low-hanging clouds glow malevolently crimson as curtains of fire shimmer across the land and fountains of incandescent liquid rock spurt hundreds of feet in the air. When Pele rages in the night, the setting is straight out of Dante's *Inferno.*

Oil painting titled "Kilauea Volcano" by William Pinkney Toler, circa 1860s.

Oil painting titled "Kilauea Caldera" by Australian painter and traveler Ernest William Christmas, circa 1916. Christmas stopped in Hawai'i on his way back to Australia from San Francisco, having exhibited his work across the United States, and fell in love with the islands. He became friends with Louis von Tempsky of Haleakala Ranch and lived on Maui for over two years before his death in 1918. He was buried at Oahu Cemetery in Honolulu.

Such is the empire of Pele, located in the southeastern part of the Island of Hawai'i, largest island in the Hawaiian Chain. Though her permanent home is the Halema'uma'u fire pit within the caldera of Kīlauea, her province includes a major section of the island.

South and east of Hilo lies the district of Puna, scene of many so-called "rift zone" eruptions. When pressure builds up in Kīlauea, it is often relieved when lava flows eastward underground through conduits and areas of weakness, only to erupt in Puna, many miles from Kīlauea. The region is dotted with cinder cones and lava flows from recent eruptions, some of which reach the sea and add new land. In early 1960, the Puna village of Kapoho was buried by a lava flow that also added 500 new acres to the island.

What Pele generously adds, she can just as capriciously take away. On November 29, 1975, Halapē Park on the coast below Kīlauea sank several feet, causing the sea to rush in and cover acres of land with several feet of water. This sinking of coastal land was accompanied by severe earthquakes, landslides, tidal waves, and a brief outburst of volcanic eruption in Kīlauea. There were two fatalities resulting from the disastrous combination of events. Property damage on the Big Island ran into millions of dollars. The earthquakes, in diminishing severity, were strong enough to wake people up at 3 a.m. on the Island of Maui.

South from Kīlauea lies the district of Kaʻū; southernmost province of the Big Island and once a kingdom in its own right. Before Kamehameha the Great united Hawaiʻi as a nation, the Hawaiian Islands were divided into a series of petty kingdoms that were constantly at war with each other. Usually, each major island was a separate kingdom but, because of its huge size, the island of Hawaiʻi was often segmented into three or more kingdoms. During Kamehameha's conquest of the Big Island, the kingdom of Kaʻū was the last to surrender.

Keōua's Army

According to some students of Hawaiian history, Pele intervened directly in island political affairs of that time. During one of the many battles for control of the Island, the forces of Kaʻū, un-

Lava flow at Hawaiʻi Volcanoes National Park on Hawaiʻi Island. SHANE MYERS | DREAMSTIME.COM

Oil painting titled "Kilauea by Day" by Titian Ramsay Peale, circa 1842. In 1838, Peale served as chief naturalist for the United States Exploring Expedition (1838–1842) led by Lt. Charles Wilkes aboard the USS Peacock, *visiting the islands in 1940.* BISHOP MUSEUM

der Keōua, were retreating from a battle against Kamehameha near Hilo. On the way back to Ka'ū, they were passing between Kīlauea and Mauna Loa when their journey was interrupted by fierce volcanic activity. The noise, smoke, and confusion panicked the army and its women and children camp-followers. Keōua decided to send his army on through, but as a safety precaution, he divided it into three separate groups. The first contingent passed safely along the trail past Kīlauea. But the second was trapped by an explosive outburst of hot ashes, mud, rock, and poisonous gases. They were found lying about, clasping their throats as if gasping for air, and with their legs still bent in a running position. The rest of the army made a safe passage but Keōua had lost one-third of his effective fighting force. The effect on the morale of the remaining Ka'ū army survivors was devastating. If the goddess Pele herself had taken sides against them, how could they resist Kamehameha? To this day, footprints of Keōua's escaping warriors are visible in ash and mud deposits they ran through in their panic-stricken dash out of Pele's domain. The ash and mud have now hardened to stone and the footprints have been preserved as a testament to the wrath of Pele.

PELE'S HIGH MOUNTAINS

View of Mauna Loa, the largest active volcano on earth looms large in the distance with cinder cones in the foreground. MNSTUDIO | DREAMSTIME.COM

Towering high above Kīlauea, Puna, and Ka'ū, the massive profile of Mauna Loa dominates the southern half of the island. This too is part of Pele's domain because Mauna Loa (Long Mountain) is an active volcano. At its top, at 13,680 feet, is the crater of Moku'āweoweo (island of lurid burning) which has erupted every few years during the past two centuries or more. Since 1950, it has been fairly quiet, though there have been recent small eruptions from rifts on the mountain's immense flanks. Mount Hualālai above Kailua village on the island's west coast completes the listing of Pele's volcanic territory on the Big Island. Hualālai has not erupted since 1801 but is still considered to be "alive" since a century or two is only a moment in the life of a volcano.

ERUPTIONS

The Hawaiians of old saw volcanic activity as concrete evidence of Pele's handiwork, whereas modern geologists have a somewhat different explanation. Hawai'i's major volcanoes are of a type known as shield volcanoes, which are broad, gently sloped mountains shaped like a saucer turned upside down. They are the products of outpourings of very hot and very liquid lavas that often flow fifteen or twenty miles before solidifying. The more typical cone-shaped volcanoes, such as Vesuvius and Fujiyama, have been built up from viscous or "sticky" lava which flows very slowly and tends to build

A photo showing how close one could stand next to Halema'uma'u taken by Brother Bertram Gabriel Bellinghausen who was the first director of Saint Louis College on O'ahu. circa 1883. CHAMINADE UNIVERSITY

steeper slopes than those found on Hawaiian volcanoes. Eruptions from Hawai'i's shield volcanoes are comparatively gentle and safe in contrast to the explosive nature of eruptions from their cone-shaped cousins in other parts of the world. Kīlauea is probably the only "drive-in volcano" in the world, so safe that a road leads down into the caldera. Visitors may drive down to look into the fire pit of Halema'uma'u in complete safety.

The mechanism of volcanic eruptions is only partially understood, but at least the basic process is known. Kīlauea Volcano is the site of intensive studies by scientists from all over the world and has provided invaluable information about the structure and mechanism of volcanoes in general. Such studies indicate that eruptions begin when magma rises through a system of tubes or conduits from a region some thirty-five miles down in the earth's mantle. Magma rises because it consists of molten rock saturated with gases, and this material is lighter than the overlying rock. About two miles beneath Kīlauea's summit, the magma fills a reservoir and then forces its way through fissures and cracks to erupt on the surface, usually within the crater. Some of the magma surfaces along rift zones (lines of weakness) which extend outward from the summit toward the sea. An imminent eruption often warns of its coming by an increase in the frequency and severity of localized earthquakes. The dome of the mountain also swells and rises due to the pressure of upwelling lava, and the summit of Kīlauea is often raised as much as five feet. The swelling of the mountain is measured by a device known as a tilt meter, while seismographs record the increasing earthquake activity.

HALEMAʻUMAʻU CRATER

Pele's current residence is reputed to lie deep down in the pit crater of Halemaʻumaʻu in the center of Kīlauea's caldera. In the Hawaiian language, the name Halemaʻumaʻu means, "House of Ferns." Since there are no ferns now growing on the barren crater walls, the name would appear to be inappropriate. But Hawaiians explain this seeming contradiction by the fact that, long before the first Europeans came to Hawaiʻi, there were two crater pits inside Kīlauea. One was as free of plant life as the present crater, but the other had ʻamaʻumaʻu ferns growing on its walls. Then, during an explosive eruption, the two pits became one large pit. The memory of the long ago ferns persists in the crater's name.

View of Kīlauea within hours of an eruption with ʻamaʻu ferns in the foreground.
J. WEI | NATIONAL PARK SERVICE

PELE AND THE MISSIONARIES

Reverend William Ellis (1794–1872). WISBECH & FENLAND MUSEUM

The first known white men to visit Pele's domain were a party of four missionaries engaged in a walking expedition around the island of Hawai'i. They hoped to visit every village and settlement of any consequence and so to spread the gospel among the inhabitants, the majority of whom had heard only rumors about the new religion which had come to Hawai'i only a few years before.

After passing through Ka'ū, the group, headed by Reverend William Ellis, trekked across difficult lava-strewn terrain toward Pele's home in Kīlauea. Nearing the great caldera, the missionaries noticed some low bushes, bearing red and yellow berries, which their Hawaiian guides called 'ōhelo. The hungry and thirsty missionaries eagerly plucked and ate every berry they could find. As soon as their guides noticed what they were doing, they begged the missionaries to cease, saying that they were now entering Pele's dominion and that the berries were sacred to her. It was forbidden to eat them until some had been offered to her and her permission had been asked. As Ellis' Journal tells it, "Some of them said, 'We are afraid. We shall be overtaken by some calamity before we leave this place.' We advised them to dismiss their fears, and eat with us, as we knew they were thirsty and faint. They shook their heads, and perceiving us determined to disregard their entreaties, walked along in silence."

Later, when the party had reached the rim of Kīlauea's caldera, Ellis continued his remarks about the 'ōhelo. "As we passed along, we observed the natives, who had hitherto refused to touch any of the ʻōhelo berries, now gathered several bunches, and, after offering a part to Pele, eat them very freely."

The party descended into the caldera toward the edge of Halemaʻumaʻu fire pit. Ellis and his party were literally awestruck, a condition that many a modern visitor to Kīlauea can understand. Again, from Ellis' Journal, "We at length came to the edge of the great crater, where a spectacle, sublime and even appalling, presented itself before us—'We stopped, and trembled.'—Astonishment and awe for some moments rendered us mute, and like statues, we stood fixed to the spot, with our eyes riveted on the abyss below.—The bottom was covered with lava, and the southwest and northern parts of it were one vast flood of burning matter, in a state of terrific ebullition, rolling to and fro its 'fiery surge' and flaming billows."

Watercolor painting titled "Interior of the Great Crater of Kilauea, Mauna Loa, Hawaii, Sandwich Islands" painted by George French Angas, circa 1852. AUCKLAND MUSEUM

HOW PELE CAME TO KĪLAUEA

According to old Hawaiian legends, Pele did not always live in the Hawaiian Islands, but originally came from a far off land called Kalakeenuiakane from which she had been driven by her sister Namakaokahai. With her youngest sister Hi‘iaka, Pele went in search of a new land described to her by Namakaokahai's husband.

Pele's Hawaiian odyssey began on Kaua‘i, the first Hawaiian island she found after the journey from her homeland. She had brought along her magic digging stick to excavate the kind of home she preferred, a deep pit high atop a mountain of lava. The rock of Kaua‘i's interior was too hard even for Pele's powerful digging stick, so she tried again in the coastal lowlands. But no sooner had she dug a suitable crater than the sea goddess caused water to rush in and extinguish the hot fires that were Pele's idea of a comfortable atmosphere.

Frustrated on Kaua‘i, the fire goddess moved to O‘ahu, where she dug and built a huge flaming crater at what is now known as Diamond Head. Once again, the sea flowed in and doused the underground flames of Pele's home.

Aerial view showing interior of Diamond Head crater. WINDWARDSKIES | *Dreamstime.com*

Oil painting titled "Halemaumau Crater, Kilauea, Hawaii" painted by Lionel Walden, circa 1915, a Connecticut artist who first visited the islands in 1911.
AMERICAN EAGLE FINE ART

And so, Pele moved through the islands one by one—Moloka'i, Lāna'i, Kaho'olawe, and Maui—digging a home and sooner or later meeting defeat from the infiltrating waters the sea goddess sent to torment her.

Hawaiian place names throughout the islands chronicle her peregrinations in such localities as Kaua'i's Pu'u-o-Pele (the hill of Pele), O'ahu's Ka Lua o Pele (the pit of Pele), and Maui's No Iwi o Pele (the bones of Pele), where Pele fought the sea goddess so fiercely that, though she survived, she left some of her bones behind.

Finally Pele came to the Island of Hawai'i, a giant land where she could select a site far from the sea and be left in peace. At last she found the perfect spot and dug herself a palatial home in the fire pit of Halema'uma'u inside Kīlauea's caldera.

In the long ages of geological time, Pele may some day be on the move again. Off the southeastern coast of Hawai'i, submarine volcanoes are slowly building up from the ocean floor. One day they may break above the surface of the ocean and a new Hawaiian island may make its debut upon the scene. Pele will be there, busy and angry as ever, while her fiery outbursts build the land ever higher and higher.

Drawing of Queen Ka'ahumanu by Louis Choris, a Russian painter who traveled to the islands aboard the Rurik *with Captain Otto von Kotzebue in 1816.* HAWAI'I STATE ARCHIVES

A Priestess of Pele

The Reverend Ellis and his group did not actually meet up with a priest or priestess of Pele, but their cavalier attitude toward the practices associated with the volcano goddess were bound to stimulate a reaction from Pele's still faithful priesthood. Some months after the missionaries' visit to Kīlauea, a priestess of Pele arrived in Lahaina, Maui, then the residence of most of the high chiefs of Hawai'i. She must have been a bizarre sight, her robes gathered around her, all the edges of which were burnt with fire. Carrying a staff in her hand, she was preceded by her daughter who was an acolyte for the priesthood. Thousands of curious people followed to witness her audience with the chiefs, who had asked her to state her problem.

The priestess of Pele told the assembled chiefs that in a vision she had talked with Pele who had charged her to complain to the chiefs that some foreigners had visited Kīlauea, eaten the sacred 'ōhelo berries, thrown stones into her crater home, and had committed many other acts of desecration. In the vision, Pele had warned that if these foreigners were not banished from the islands, Pele would avenge this insult by covering the entire Island with lava and destroying all the people. The bystanders were almost as astonished as the priestess herself when Ka'ahumanu, the kuhina nui or premier, and widow of Kamehameha the Great, ordered that the sacred objects and other paraphernalia of the priestess be thrown into the fire. Ka'ahumanu told the priestess that her so-called vision was a lie and ordered her to return home and cease deceiving the people. In this action, Ka'ahumanu was supported by the council of chieftains. It must have been gratifying to the missionaries to see this action taken without missionary participation, which would have subjected them to accusations of having directed the chiefs in their decision.

Hiram Bingham preaching to Queen Ka'ahumanu in Waimea, 1826. Etching from his book, A Residence of Twenty-one Years in the Sandwich Islands.

Chiefess Kapi'olani defying Pele, painted for Amfac, Inc. by Peter Hurd.

A Chiefess Defies Pele

It was all very well for foreigners to defy Pele and ignore the practices and kapu surrounding her cult, but it was another matter for a Hawaiian to do so. Although the Hawaiian religion had been formally abolished by King Kamehameha II in 1820, the

common people still clung tenaciously to many of their beliefs, particularly those concerning the ferocious Pele, most feared divinity on the Island of Hawaiʻi. Devotees of the goddess told the people that, while the foreigners might be exempt from Pele's vengeance, she would tolerate no disrespect from the Hawaiian people. It would take a fearless Hawaiian indeed to defy a goddess, the unmistakable signs of whose fury were everywhere evident.

There was such a bold and courageous Hawaiian and her name was Kapi'olani. She was the wife of Naihe, a chief of the Puna district, and she was a convert to Christianity. (A later namesake was Queen Kapi'olani, wife of King Kalākaua.) Chiefess Kapi'olani's defiance of Pele grew out of her great love for Christianity. Her own conversion did not seem to her to be sufficient to satisfy her deep religious convictions; she desired to spread these beliefs among her own people. She saw far too many of her people, especially those in Puna and Ka'ū, continue to worship the fearsome volcano goddess. If they were ever to see the light as she had, then she knew that she must break the spell of Pele over her people. They must learn to pray to Jehovah, not to Pele.

The Puna and Ka'ū districts were closest to Kīlauea and were noted for frequent volcanic disturbances. It was there, more than anywhere, that the people worshipped the fierce goddess. Accordingly, Kapi'olani set out on a self-imposed mission to publicly defy Pele. In December 1824, she journeyed to Kīlauea accompanied by many friends and attendants. They begged her not to make such a dangerous trip, certain to bring down the wrath of bad-tempered Pele. Kapi'olani replied, "If I am destroyed, you may all believe in Pele. If I am not destroyed, you must all turn to the only true God."

A Caucasian depiction of Chiefess Kapi'olani defying Pele from The Romance of Missionary Heroism *by John Chrisholm Lambert, 1907.*

Strong in her faith, she walked to the brink of the fire pit. A priestess of Pele came up to the chiefess and warned her not to go on. The priestess carried what she claimed to be a letter from Pele. She read the so-called "letter," a confused diatribe of warnings and baleful threats obviously made up as she went along. Kapi'olani replied by reading biblical passages in the Hawaiian language (she had learned to read and write from the missionaries), the implication being that the "letter" of the priestess was a sheer fabrication. Then, dismissing the priestess, Kapi'olani descended into the smoldering crater. To symbolize her defiance of Pele, she ate the sacred 'ōhelo berries without seeking prior permission, and she flung stones into the boiling mass of lava.

As she threw the stones, she is said to have shouted, "I do not fear Pele. Should I perish by her wrath, then you may fear her power. But if Jehovah saves me while I am breaking her tabus, then you must fear and love him." When the Reverend William Ellis heard of Kapi'olani's act, he wrote in his journal, "What effect the conduct of Kapi'olani, on this occasion, will have on the natives in general, remains yet to be discovered."

The poet Tennyson immortalized her defiant act in a poem published in 1893. The six stanza poem describes Kapi'olani's accomplishment in breaking the hold of Pele on her people and in strengthening the cause of Christianity among them. The poem's last stanza sums up her heroic gesture.

One from the Sunrise
Dawn'd on His people, and slowly before him
Vanish'd shadow-like
Gods and Goddesses.
None but the terrible Pele remaining as Kapiolani ascended her mountain,
Baffled her priesthood,
Broke the Taboo,
Dipt to the Crater,
Called on the power adored by the Christian, and crying "I dare her, let Pele avenge herself!"
Into the flame-billow dash'd the berries, and
drove the demon from Hah-wy-ee.

PELE—DOWN, BUT NOT OUT

The first Christian missionaries to arrive in Hawai'i were lucky compared to their counterparts in other regions of Oceania. Those who carried Christianity to Polynesia and Melanesia had to face opposition from ancient and firmly entrenched native religions, an opposition that sometimes took a violent turn. But in Hawai'i they encountered something totally unexpected and, from the missionary viewpoint, very fortunate. In an act almost without parallel in the known history of the world, the Hawaiians had overthrown their own religion shortly after the death of Kamehameha the Great in 1819.

Expecting to fight the good fight against "heathenish idolatry," the travel-weary missionaries debarked in a land without religion. Kū, Kanaloa, Lono, Kāne—the great gods and the host of demigods, family gods, and lesser spirits—all had lost their hold over the minds of Hawai'i's people. It was as if Providence had offered Hawai'i to the missionaries as a gift. But the gift was flawed by

Sketch by William Ellis showing the journey of the missionaries through Pele's domain, circa 1827. Ellis and his group made little headway bringing Christianity into the land of the fire goddess.

an important exception. Pele and her cult were still alive and well, a very robust fly in the missionary ointment.

Princess Ruth Ke'elikōlani who saved Hilo from Pele's wrath, pictured here with Samuel Parker and John Adams Cummins, circa 1877. HAWAI'I STATE ARCHIVES

Numerous priests and priestesses maintained the ceremonial aspects of Pele's cult intact. Both they and the goddess were respected and feared by the people, particularly on the Island of Hawai'i. These beliefs and practices discomfited the missionaries, who naturally wished to root them out as symbols of the still weak influence of their Christian teachings. Thousands of Hawaiians were willing to accept the new religion but still held Pele in secret awe. And why not? They could see evidence of Pele's destructive handiwork on every side. Hardly an acre of their lands existed that was not associated with some ancient legend of the fiery volcano goddess.

When Ellis and his group traveled through the Ka'ū and Kīlauea regions, they often admonished the Hawaiian guides for their strict adherence to certain customs and prohibitions while in Pele's domain.

Pele's hold on the popular imagination was so strong that even after the Chiefess Kapi'olani boldly defied the goddess, Ellis wondered whether even this courageous act would have any long-lasting effect. It would be natural to assume that once Christianity had taken firm hold, Pele and the beliefs associated with her would gradually fade away. But this was not to be.

In 1880, giant Mauna Loa erupted. An immense lava flow advanced relentlessly downhill toward the city of Hilo, threatening to destroy the city and perhaps fill in the harbor upon which Hilo depended as a port. When the lava river approached Hilo's outskirts, many desperate Hawaiians sought the help of Princess Ruth Ke'elikōlani, one of the last of the Kamehameha dynasty and an imposing woman in her own right. Princess Ruth took the first available boat from Honolulu to Hilo, where she then went to the edge of the flow which was now very close to the city. The noblewoman, summoning up all the divine authority of her sacred ali'i ancestry, intoned ancient chants to Pele and threw various gifts onto the hot lava in an effort to soften the goddess' anger. The next day, the lava flow suddenly stopped and the city of Hilo was spared.

On April 10, 1926, a rift crack at the 7600-foot level of Mauna Loa's western flank began pouring out huge amounts of fast-moving lava which raced down the slope toward the sea. High above, at 13,000 feet inside the caldera of Moku'āweoweo, there was a simultaneous but short-lived eruption. The lavas from this summit eruption remained within the caldera. But the flank eruption was a major one which lasted for fourteen days and, before it was over, had poured out 150,000,000 cubic yards of lava that covered an area of more than thirteen square miles.

Those are the bare statistics. But as ever when dealing with the works of Pele, statistics alone do not tell the full story. Everything she does is dramatic and has some impact on the lives of those who call the Big Island home.

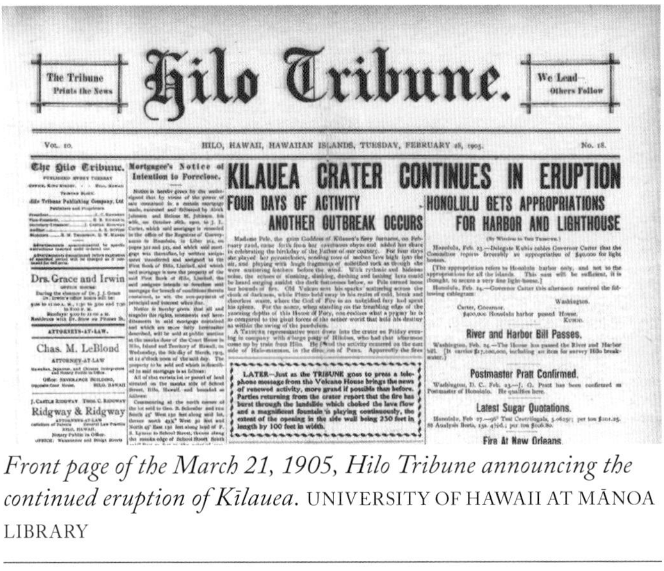
The Tribune Prints the News

Hilo Tribune.

We Lead—Others Follow

Vol. 10. HILO, HAWAII, HAWAIIAN ISLANDS, TUESDAY, FEBRUARY 28, 1905. No. 18.

The Hilo Tribune.

Mortgagee's Notice of Intention to Foreclose.

KILAUEA CRATER CONTINUES IN ERUPTION

FOUR DAYS OF ACTIVITY

ANOTHER OUTBREAK OCCURS

LATER—Just as the TRIBUNE goes to press a telephone message from the Volcano House brings the news of renewed activity, more grand if possible than before. Parties returning from the crater report that the fire has burst through the landslide which choked the lava flow and a magnificent fountain is playing continuously, the extent of the opening in the side wall being 250 feet in length by 100 feet in width.

HONOLULU GETS APPROPRIATIONS FOR HARBOR AND LIGHTHOUSE

River and Harbor Bill Passes.

Postmaster Pratt Confirmed.

Latest Sugar Quotations.

Fire At New Orleans

Drs. Grace and Irwin

ATTORNEYS-AT-LAW.

Chas. M. LeBlond

ATTORNEY-AT-LAW

Ridgway & Ridgway

Front page of the March 21, 1905, Hilo Tribune announcing the continued eruption of Kīlauea. UNIVERSITY OF HAWAII AT MĀNOA LIBRARY

THE FURY OF PELE

Far down on the western shore lay the small village of Hoʻōpūloa at the head of a tiny harbor. At first, the inhabitants felt little anxiety since the odds were unlikely that any particular flow would endanger their village. But soon, apprehension began to grow. On the slopes above the village, a black and menacing stain was spreading across the landscape, widening as it advanced. There was no denying that the general direction of the dark and inexorable movement was now definitely toward Hoʻōpūloa.

At 5:15 in the morning of April 18, the front of the wide lava flow had actually entered the village and the first of its homes caught fire from the intense heat as the clinkery mass touched its flimsy walls. So, just eight days after the fissure had opened high up on Mauna Loa, it was all over for the village of Hoʻōpūloa. Like an irresistible juggernaut, the lava overwhelmed the tiny collection of homes and small commercial buildings one by one until nothing was left.

The villagers had been allowed plenty of time to evacuate their homes and to save most of their belongings. But many stayed on the sidelines to watch, in the vain hope that the lava would halt its advance somewhat short of complete destruction. Pele's conquering horde not only swept away the village in its path, but entered the ocean and added a quarter of a mile of new land to what had once been a snug harbor. When the eruption had finally run its course, both Hoʻōpūloa and its harbor had been wiped off the face of the earth.

PELE SMOTHERS KAPOHO TOWN

Even today, there remains a strong undercurrent of respect and fear of Pele's unpredictable destructiveness. In 1955, fissures opened in the eastern rift zone of Kīlauea, in the middle of cane fields and papaya groves near the small Puna village of Kapoho. Long curtains of fire leaped up and spread ash and lava over the surrounding countryside. Eventually, lava began to pour forth in great quantities, posing a threat to the village. The people of Kapoho, like those of Hilo in an earlier day, attempted to appease Pele's fury in the hope that the village would be spared. They chanted the ancient invocations and offered her the fruits of the land as well as gifts of pork and alcoholic beverages. But unlike the efforts of Princess Ruth in the Hilo of old, it was all to no avail. Slowly and relentlessly, the village of Kapoho was buried under ash and creeping lava flows.

Pele Takes on the U.S. Army

Unlikely as it may seem, Pele has several times come into conflict with the armed forces of the United States. The first confrontation came in 1935, when an eruption sent lava streams racing down the slopes of Mauna Loa toward the city of Hilo. Daily, it became more obvious that the city was endangered by the inexorable advance of lava. Island authorities hastily conferred with experts from the Volcano Observatory at Kīlauea and with U.S. Army officials. They decided to try something new to bomb selected areas in front of the approaching lava flow in an attempt to divert it away from Hilo itself.

The lava flow from Mauna Loa on December 30, 1935, traveled 600 feet in twenty-five minutes. NATIONAL PARK SERVICE

The U.S. Army Air Corps was called into action and it dropped 600-pound bombs on sectors designated by the volcanologists. Seemingly, this tactic proved successful as the lava changed course and Hilo was saved once again. Some observers disagreed, stating that the bombs had little or no real effect on the course of the lava streams.

A bomb dropped on the 1935 Mauna Loa Humuʻula lava flow was found in 1939 during Thomas Jaggar's post-eruption inspection of the flow. US GEOLOGICAL SURVEY (USGS)

In 1942, the Army Air Corps was brought in again to bomb Pele's flaming rivers and attempt to divert them away from inhabited places. Once more, the effectiveness of this procedure was doubted by many experts. In any case, Pele didn't give up so easily. She had a more serious defiance of the armed forces still up her sleeve.

This eruption occurred shortly after the Pearl Harbor attack and a blackout regulation was in force throughout the Islands. The blackout was rigidly enforced but there was one glaring exception to the rule. Every night Pele's fires lit up the sky over the Big Island, providing a bright beacon for enemy ships, submarines, or airplanes which might be navigating toward the Hawaiian Islands. Here was one night light the military could not extinguish no matter what dire penalties they might threaten. What could they do? Arrest Pele?

Steam explosion in Halemaʻumaʻu on May 22, 1924, as seen from Volcano House.
PHOTO BY TAI SING LOO. NATIONAL PARK SERVICE

1924 EXPLOSIONS

Kapoho residents in lower Puna await evacuation during seismic tremors prior to the 1924 eruption at Kīlauea's summit. Photo by Maehara, Kenichi. NATIONAL PARK SERVICE

For at least a century prior to 1924, Kīlauea had been the scene of almost continuous activity. But it was activity of a benign nature. The lava lake inside Halema'uma'u put on a constant show of glowing red lava to the delight of awed visitors. The level of the lava lake rose and fell through the years, occasionally spilling over into the caldera itself and, on rare occasions, slight flows ran out beyond Kīlauea through gaps in the wall. But the one constant was that Kīlauea was a volcano whose activities could be viewed in almost complete safety.

The eruptions in the spring of 1924 were to show Pele at her most dangerous. People had almost been lulled into a false sense of security by the fact that there had not been a single human fatality at Kīlauea in more than a century. But scientists at the Volcano Observatory were aware that even the "safest" volcano held an awesome potential for destruction.

In April of 1924 the scientific observers were alerted to the possibility that something major was brewing, although there was no way of foretelling exactly what would happen. In that month an almost continuous series of earth tremors began in the rift zone to the east of Kīlauea. At Kapoho Village, which was later destroyed in the rift eruptions of 1960, at least 200 earthquakes strong enough to be felt occurred on April 22 and 23.

A number of the earthquakes were very strong. Cracks opened and closed in the ground. In one case, a cow fell into one of these chasms and was killed when the crack closed and crushed the poor animal to death. A famous photograph taken at the time shows the

Explosive eruption column from Halema'uma'u Crater at 11:15 a.m. on May 18, 1924, just one of many in a series of similar events during May 11-27. Photo from northwest rim of Kīlauea summit. MAEHARA, K. | USGS

cow's legs protruding from the ground. The coastline near Cape Kumukahi sank fourteen feet and the ocean invaded the land to a distance of almost half a mile.

All the while, the lava lake inside Halema'uma'u was sinking rapidly. On May 13, strong explosions inside the crater flung hot boulders high into the air. Suddenly the rim of Halema'uma'u was no longer a spot for visitors to look down into but became a very dangerous place to be. The superintendent of the national park service closed the crater area to visitors, and probably just in time to prevent great loss of life. Traditionally, an eruption of Kīlauea attracts crowds of sightseers and, had they been allowed near the crater, there would have been many killed and injured. Even so, there were minor injuries reported that day from the flying debris and the superintendent himself was knocked over by the bombardment.

On that day the *Honolulu Advertiser* headed its story on developments as follows: BARRAGE OF ROCKS FROM KILAUEA SHOOT 2000 FEET FROM RIM, Superintendent Boles Stops

Thomas A. Jaggar, Jr., long time director of HVO, examining a boulder weighing approximately 12 tons that was thrown out by the volcano in one of its moments of extreme fury on May 18, 1924. TAI SING LOO | USGS

Sightseers Near Crater Just Before Countryside Is Stormed With 300-Pound Boulders.

The explosive activity reached its climax on May 18. Huge, towering clouds of dust rose more than 20,000 feet above the crater and the surrounding countryside was showered with rains of mud, pebbles, and boulders. An eight-ton boulder still lies where it fell, about one-fourth of a mile from the pit of Halema'uma'u.

On May 18, the *Honolulu Advertiser* ran this story:

VOLCANO HOUSE, KILAUEA, MAY 18.

Halemaumau has been at its most violent stage of the present disturbance during the past 12 hours, and continues with its terrific eruptions, exploding rocks and showers sand and ashes almost incessantly. Eruptions occur at various intervals, the fifth one during the past several days, taking place shortly after 11 o'clock last night and another at 3 o'clock this morning. A few minutes past 11 o'clock today, the greatest outbreak yet recorded sent giant white-hot boulders high into the air.

At noon another outbreak took place, but it was in miniature proportion to the earlier eruptions. Similar ones are taking place at irregular intervals.

ELEMENTS LEND WRATH

Each large eruption is accompanied by a shower of rocks of immense size, hurled to a distance of almost three-quarters of a mile. They are followed by a downpour of ashes and mud caused by the tremendous rainfall. The elements also lend their wrath to the spectacle as bolts of lightning and violent thunder crack and rumble through the smoke columns.

Truman A. Taylor, Pahala bookkeeper, witnessing the eruptions at a distance of approximately 1800 feet from the pit, was struck down by rocks, had both legs crushed and was partially burned by hot ash. Taylor was found shortly before noon, partly covered by burning ash, by an unidentified man who was attracted by screams for help. Captain P.J. McKenzie, surgeon of the Kilauea military camp, gave first aid and rushed Taylor to the Hilo hospital in an army ambulance. Miss Molly Thomas, Hilo nurse, accompanied him.

SOLDIERS MISSING

Two soldiers, visiting at the military camp, were seen at the edge of the pit on the north side, shortly before the giant explosion took place at 11 o'clock this morning, and have not been accounted for since. Captain Charles H. Perkins, 35th Infantry, officer in charge of the army camp, with a large searching party, were headed down Uwekahuna Bluff gulch this afternoon. But no reports from them had been received up to late this afternoon.

Thomas Jaggar standing next to newly-formed cracks in the aftermath of the May 1924 eruption, looking east-northeast toward Kīlauea Iki. TAI SING LOO | USGS

The injured man was within the prescribed danger zone when struck down by the rocks, it was learned.

The missing soldiers later turned up unharmed, but Mr. Taylor, who had been felled by rocks and burned by ash, died on the way to Hilo Hospital. He was so intent on photographing the eruption that he lost his own natural sense of caution and ignored warnings ordering people to stay clear of the crater area. The park superintendent closed the entire Volcano national park to visitors. At Volcano House, only two men remained on duty, watching developments, and Kilauea army camp was temporarily abandoned.

Thus, Pele, who had shown only her peaceful side for over a century, suddenly revealed the side of her personality that the ancient Hawaiians had feared through the long ages of her reign over Kilauea.

Volcano House Hotel circa 1866 at the edge of Kīlauea Volcano as it looked when Mark Twain visited. NATIONAL PARK SERVICE (NPS)

VOLCANO HOUSE

One of the world's most unique hotels is Volcano House, situated on the very rim of Kīlauea. Guests eat and drink in comfort while enjoying a panoramic view of the caldera, Halema'uma'u fire pit, and the awe-inspiring scenery. Because of its unusual location, Volcano House can only be compared with such one-of-its-kind inns as Kenya's Tree Tops.

Since time immemorial, there has been a place of rest for weary travelers through Pele's empire. Long before the arrival of Captain Cook's expedition, Hawaiians who passed through the region of Kīlauea would camp on the caldera's northern rim, building a rude shelter of small tree trunks and ferns, thatched with grass, as protection from the chill and mists of the night. These huts were intended only for overnight use and were naturally quite flimsy. The next traveling party to come along would repair the hut rather than build a new one. This happened so frequently that the structures eventually became more permanent and spacious.

The earliest known foreigners to spend the night in such a hut beside Kīlauea were the Reverend Ellis and his group of missionaries, who passed the night of August 1, 1823, there in the company of their Hawaiian guides. Ellis and his companions were not too happy with its location, as the hut was built only four feet from the edge of the precipice on unstable ground that looked as if it might fall into the crater at any moment. But try as they might, they were unable to convince their guides to build a hut at another, safer-appearing location. According to the Hawaiian guides, this was the only safe location as it was the one permitted by Pele herself, and that to sleep anywhere else would indeed be dangerous due to the risk of offending the goddess.

A much larger Hawaiian dwelling was built in 1824 to accommodate Chiefess Kapi'olani on her famed visit with the avowed purpose of defying Pele. This house was erected on the ridge between Kīlauea and Kīlauea Iki craters. It was used a short time later by an exploring party from H.M.S. *Blonde* under Captain Lord Byron, who had brought the bodies of King Liholiho and Queen Kamāmalu back to Hawai'i after their tragic deaths in London. This ridge is known today as Byron Ledge and it is understandable if people think it was named after the famed poet, Lord Byron. Captain Lord Byron was a cousin of the poet and had inherited the title upon the poet's death.

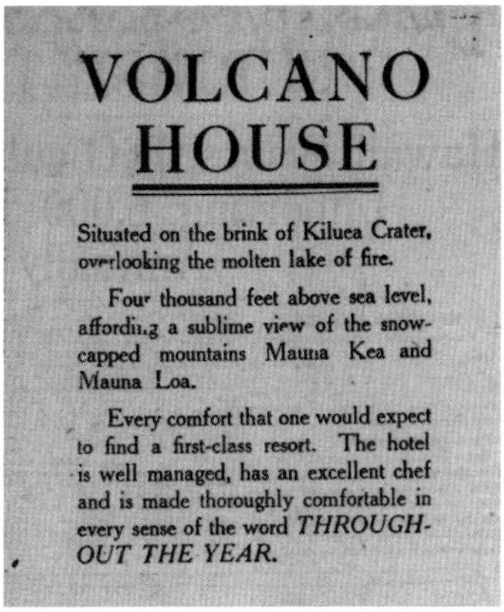

An ad promoting the unique location and amenities of Volcano House in The San Francisco Call, *August 14, 1912.* UH MĀNOA LIBRARY.

With the ever-increasing flow of visitors to the volcano, the rude shelters gradually grew or were rebuilt until they became quite large. Before long, they were in private hands and the beginnings of an inn or hotel concept were evident in the charging of a tariff and the provision of meals. Volcano House first became officially known by that name in the 1840s when a larger and improved grass house was built by Benjamin Pittman for the accommodation of travelers. Pittman supervised the shelter (it was not yet a true hotel) and even supplied a guest book or register for visitors.

Volcano House in Kīlauea, circa 1912. PHOTO BY ROBERT K. BONINE, LIBRARY OF CONGRESS

Volcano House grew into a large thatched structure capable of accommodating about forty visitors, according to Princess Lili'uokalani (later Queen), who spent a night there in the early 1860s.

Members of the Los Angeles Chamber of Commerce pose in front of Volcano House in 1907. CALIFORNIA HISTORICAL SOCIETY COLLECTION

It was inevitable that an enterprising businessman would become aware of Kīlauea's potential as a profit-making tourist attraction. In 1866, Julius C. Richardson, in partnership with owners of

A crowd of visitors from the steamships Haleakalā *and* Matsonia *pose at their own risk in front of the Volcano House Hote with a large eruption plume in the background.* PHOTO BY TAI SING LOO. USGS

a nearby ranch, built a grass-thatched cottage with four bedrooms, a parlor, and a dining room. Volcano House, however primitive by modern standards, was now a genuine hotel. One of its first prominent guests was Mark Twain, who was obviously pleased at the unexpected comfort found in so remote a place. In an 1866 letter to the *Sacramento Union,* he wrote, "The surprise of finding a good hotel in such an outlandish spot startled me considerably more than the volcano did. The house is new—built three or four months ago—and the table is good."

With the passage of time, Volcano House was rebuilt and improved several times. The first really substantial building was erected in 1891, a two-story frame building with fourteen rooms. The older building was retained as an annex to the new Volcano House, and forty or more guests could be accommodated in comfort. Throughout the years, Volcano House was host to dignitaries from all over the world, as well as everyday travelers and tourists. Its guest register became a fascinating collection of signatures and comments by kings, princes, presidents, statesmen, and other prominent persons

Gifts left for Pele on hardened lava.
GEORGE BURBA | DREAMSTIME.COM

entered over the last hundred years or more. Today's hostelry blends the most modern conveniences with the unique Hawaiian country-style inn atmosphere that has always been its hallmark.

Naturally, a hotel so intimately related to Pele's home will have its own stories to tell and even customs influenced by the great volcano and its celebrated inhabitant. "Uncle George" Lycurgus, the colorful Greek manager of Volcano House in the first half of this century, believed that gin was one of Pele's favorite gifts. No one is quite sure why he held that belief, but he religiously presented Pele with flasks of the potent libation on Mother's Day, Christmas, and New Year's.

Mr. Al Pelayo, who followed as manager, continued the tradition. On these occasions he descended into the caldera to the edge of Halema'uma'u and lowered the offerings into Pele's fire pit residence.

It goes without saying that volcanic activity is good for business at Volcano House. Shortly after the first offering of gin, eruptions began after a long period of quiet and have steadily continued. Pelayo himself has had an experience that would make one less liable to scoff at the idea of Pele as a living presence. For some months after his arrival at Volcano House, he lived alone in a nearby cabin. During the night, his door would be suddenly flung open, waking him from a sound sleep. Suspecting prowlers, he kept a shotgun near the bed. The strange happenings continued throughout his seven month residence in the cabin. After a time, it became obvious that no human or animal intruders were involved, and Pelayo resigned himself to saying, "Welcome!" to Pele's presence and going back to sleep. Geologist friends have suggested to him that the cabin may be built over an area that swells with the movement and pressures of underground lava movements, but he is not convinced.

Thomas Jaggar, director of the Hawaiian Volcano Observatory from 1912 to 1940 measures lava at Halema'uma'u in 1917 with Norton Twigg-Smith, Lorrin Thurston, Joe Monez, and Alex Lancaster looking on. USGS

Putting Pele's Energy to Work

Hawai'i has long been a world center for the study of volcanoes because of their accessibility and comparative safety. Hawai'i Volcanoes National Park, located near Volcano House, boasts a museum complete with seismograph, specimens of volcanic phenomena, and other fascinating but easy to understand exhibits which help to acquaint the unfamiliar visitor with the nature of eruptions and volcanic energy. Much study on the nature of eruptions and tremors is also being done by members of the Hawai'i Volcano Observatory, located in a building on the western rim of Kīlauea caldera. Any and all tremors are closely monitored and investigated so as to keep abreast of the immense energies that lie beneath the earth.

New fumerole located just above the crater floor in Halema'uma'u in 2010. NPS

Ever since ancient times it has been man's dream to utilize volcanic heat—not that of the eruptions themselves but rather to make use of the boiling springs and hot steam and gas fumaroles found in many volcanic regions. Hot water springs impregnated with minerals have been popular for centuries and famed for their reputed curative powers. Iceland in the North Atlantic, an island of high volcanic activity, has long utilized the steam escaping from fumaroles to heat schools and many other public buildings. Some Japanese villages are heated in a similar manner. Hot springs in many parts of the world (the U.S., Iceland, New Zealand, and Central America to name a few) are used for washing clothes. Italy has made excellent use of its volcanic heat resources, producing electricity and extracting various chemical by-products from both the gases and mineral-laden waters and steam. The State of California is another locale where the power of underground steam is being utilized at "the Geysers" in Sonoma County.

The unique Volcano House on the edge of Kīlauea takes advantage of Pele's generosity in heating its guest rooms. Each room has a radiator which carries water heated by steam tapped from the nearby Sulphur Bank. Volcano House also boasts a steam bath where guests may cleanse and refresh themselves in a humid atmosphere heated by Pele's own fires far below.

The steam which issues from innumerable cracks and chasms in the Big Island's most active volcanic areas is believed to be caused when rain waters and underground waters come in contact with rock that is heated by underlying magma. On those rare occasions when large amounts of water make direct contact with molten underground lava, the result is more likely to be a steam explosion, short-lived and very destructive. But the more usual type of steam vent is potentially useful and may have a long life extending over many centuries.

Recent years with the shortages brought on by an ever-recurring energy crisis have seen an acceleration of interest in the potentialities of the enormous amounts of energy that can possibly be found by harnessing certain aspects of the Big Island's volcanism. Most of this experimental attention is now centered around Kīlauea and its Puna rift zone. The possibilities are great, but so are the problems. For one thing, the rock in the vicinity of Kīlauea is composed of very porous lava full of cracks formed by earthquakes. Thus, while much steam is created, it also escapes all too easily through the myriad of vents available to it. By the time this steam reaches the surface, it has hardly any pressure. Of course, it is the combination of hot steam and high pressure that offers the greatest energy potential. But scientists are not discouraged. Apparently there is an inexhaustible supply available and deeper drilling may yet reveal sources of steam trapped under high pressure in more impervious rock further down. Should these efforts be successful, it would be a bonanza for the State of Hawai'i which now depends too precariously on oil shipped in from other areas. With its own source of energy, Hawai'i would become much more self-sufficient than it is at present. It would no longer be so dependent on shipping and the caprices of the oil producing countries.

A Personal Appearance

According to old Hawaiian legends, shortly before each major eruption, Pele will appear to someone in the guise of human form. This is said to be her way of warning the people that a volcanic outburst will come at any time. In a story datelined May 14, 1924, from Wai'ōhinu in the southernmost province of Ka'ū on the Big Island, the Honolulu Advertiser reported just such an instance. A resident of Wai'ōhinu reported seeing a tall, strange but beautiful woman dressed in white and with flowing black hair. People in those tiny communities tend to know everyone on sight and this was in the days before there was any tourism to speak of in that part of the Island. Several other residents of Wai'ōhinu reported seeing the same unusual looking woman walking along country lanes in the area. She spoke to no one, but went her way and was not seen again. To a Hawaiian there is nothing remarkable about such occurrences because they have taken place consistently throughout Hawai'i's traditional oral history, and invariably they portend an impending volcanic eruption.

The literature about Hawai'i, both factual and fictional, is full of references to Pele's habit of appearing to people before an-eruption. In James A. Michener's monumental novel, *Hawaii,* there are eerily beautiful passages in which Pele materializes in the presence of Hawai'i's first Polynesian settlers, warning them of volcanic eruptions and thus securing their devotion to her worship. Basing his story on ancient tales, Michener described Pele's hair as stiff and yellow, standing out from her head—very much like the threads of volcanic glass known as Pele's hair.

Pele's Hair

This strange form of natural spun glass is a by-product of the formation of Pele's Tears. As each drop is shot by explosion from a pool of lava, it trails behind it a thin thread of the liquid lava. The thread chills in the air to a filament of golden or brown glass known as Pele's Hair. Being very light, Pele's Hair is often carried downwind many miles from the eruption site. Old Hawaiian legends say that when Pele's rage was at its height, she would tear her hair out in handfuls. Thus they explained the large quantities of Pele's Hair often found after eruptions.

Pele's Tears, composed of black basalt glass, 2014. JAMES ST. JOHN

PELE'S TEARS

Pele's Tears are drops formed from very liquid lava ejected into the air. As the drops of glowing liquefied rock fall, they tend to take on a teardrop shape before solidifying. During some eruptions, they are formed in large numbers. Pele's Tears are usually dark brown or black in color and are composed mainly of volcanic glass.

PELE ON STAGE

So pervasive is Pele's aura, she has even been written into serious stage productions. Jean Charlot, in his "Three Plays of Ancient Hawai'i," wrote two substantial scenes, featuring Pele as an old woman, into his play entitled "U'i a U'i" (Beauty meets Beauty). Pele dominates the opening and closing sequences of the drama.

PELE'S SEVERAL FORMS

In almost every story dealing with Pele's appearance to a person, she is seen as a woman—sometimes as a young and beautiful maiden or even a girl child. At other times she appears as an old hag, especially when seen near the seacoast. It is for the latter reason that those who encounter an old woman not personally known to them along a lonely stretch of road, are extremely careful to treat her with deference and respect. On occasion, Pele has been seen as a woman covered with flames, or even as if she were flame in the shape of a woman. The legends also tell of rarer appearances, usually as some kind of flaming material but not in human form. Such was the case in the experience recounted below.

A CHILD SEES PELE

Mary Kawena Pukui, anthropologist and grand old lady of Hawaiian studies, tells of an incident that occurred during her childhood, the memory of which is as clear as if it happened yesterday. As a young girl, she saw a ball of fire moving slowly from the vicinity of Kīlauea and rising up the side of giant Mauna Loa. Her older relatives and friends, who also witnessed the phenomenon, told her that it was Pele going to visit her other home in the crater of Moku'āweoweo atop Mauna Loa.

People not raised in the old Hawaiian way of thinking might attempt to explain the sight as a comparatively rare form of atmospheric electricity known as ball lightning. And, in recent years it might even be more fashionable to attribute it to the sighting of an unidentified flying object, the so-called UFOs. But to a traditional Hawaiian, completely attuned to the forces of nature all about him, there would be nothing surprising about the incident. After all, Pele was merely assuming one of the forms in which she had always appeared to mankind—as a woman, or as a flame.

Of course, it is easy to pass off such things as evidences of credulity or superstition on the part of simple country folk. It would be easy if these incidents happened only to people like that. But Honolulu's newspapers recounted a strange little drama in which the participants were modern, urban city dwellers from Honolulu. A couple on vacation on the Big Island, while driving from Kona through Ka'ū and on to Kīlauea, picked up a woman on a lonely stretch of highway above South Point. Although she accepted their offer of a ride, she said nothing but just sat quietly in the back seat of the car. After traveling several miles, the husband turned around to offer her a cigarette. They had not made any stops, yet when he turned around, the woman was not there. A few days later, Kīlauea Iki erupted in one of history's most spectacular Hawaiian eruptions, shooting incandescent lava fountains 1900 feet high.

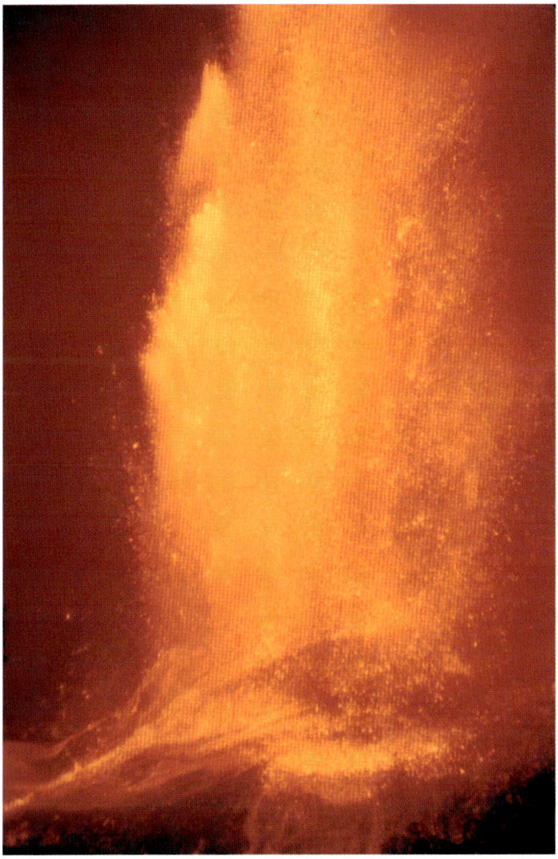

Tall lava fountain during the Kīlauea 'Ike eruption of 1959. L. PETERSON | NPS

YOU CAN'T (SHOULDN'T) TAKE IT WITH YOU

A small lava rock at Hawai'i Volcanoes National Park. LEONG CHEE ONN | DREAMSTIME.COM

It is a perfectly natural impulse for visitors to want to pick up a piece of lava as a souvenir of their visit to Pele's home. The temptation is especially strong when the lava is fresh, a glistening rich black color. After all, it would look good on the mantelpiece, it would make a handsome paperweight, and as a conversation piece it would be invaluable. What fun to tell friends and neighbors about collecting a piece of lava from a flow which had barely cooled off, then to pass it around and listen to their admiring and envious remarks.

It might be wise however, to think twice before you give in to your collecting urge. The manager of Volcano House regularly receives packages in the mail containing pieces of lava taken from Kīlauea. These packages arrive from Honolulu and from many mainland towns and cities. Almost invariably they are accompanied by a letter which describes bad luck or unfortunate occurrences that have taken place since the sender picked up the piece of lava to take home.

And they ask the manager to return the souvenir to whence it came, in the hope that this action would break their bad luck streak.

To those of a cynical frame of mind, such tales of woe are laid at the door of coincidence. But it happens often enough and with such convincing detail as to suggest that perhaps there are forces at work here that are not yet understood or that hint of the supernatural.

Whatever one's feelings on the matter, it might be for the best to restrain the impulse to take a piece of lava home from a visit to

A hiker holding cooled lava from Kīlauea in Hawai'i Volcanoes National Park. Volcanic rock is all over the Hawaiian Islands, not just Hawai'i Island—look but don't take. MARTIN MARK|DREAMSTIME.COM

Kīlauea. To many Hawaiians, the belief in Pele and the customs associated with her represent a respected part of their Polynesian heritage. To paraphrase the old traveler's saying, "When in Hawai'i, do as the Hawaiians do."

SUGGESTED READING

Andersen, Johannes Carl. *Myths & Legends of the Polynesians.* Charles E. Tuttle Company, Inc.: Rutland, Vermont & Tokyo, Japan, 1969.

Beckwith, Martha Warren. *Hawaiian Mythology.* University of Hawai'i Press: Honolulu, 1970.

Blickhahn, Harry Miller. *Uncle George of Kilauea, The Story of George Lycurgus.* Volcano House: Hawaii National Park, Hawai'i, 1961.

Brigham, William T. *The Volcanoes of Kilauea and Mauna Loa on the Island of Hawaii.* Bishop Museum Press: Honolulu, Hawai'i, 1909.

Charlot, Jean. *Three Plays of Ancient Hawaii.* University of Hawai'i Press: Honolulu, Hawaii, 1963.

Clemens, Samuel Langhorne. *Mark Twain's Letters from Hawaii.* Edited by A. Grove Day. Appleton-Century: New York, 1966.

Colum, Padraic. *Legends of Hawaii.* Yale University Press, Inc.: New Haven and London, 1937 and 1967.

Ellis, William. *Polynesian Researches: Hawaii.* Charles E. Tuttle Company, Inc.: Tokyo, Japan, 1969.

Emerson, Nathaniel Bright. *Unwritten Literature of Hawaii: The Sacred Songs of the Hula.* Charles E. Tuttle Company, Inc.: Tokyo, Japan, 1965.

Fornander, Abraham. *An Account of the Polynesian Race: Its Origins and Migrations, and the Ancient History of the Hawaiian People to the Time of Kamehameha I.* Charles E. Tuttle Company, Inc.: Rutland, Vermont & Tokyo, Japan, 1969.

Herbert, Don and Bardossi, Fulvio. *Kilauea: Case History of a Volcano.* Harper & Row: New York, 1968.

Jaggar, T.A. *Volcanoes Declare War.* Paradise of the Pacific, Ltd.: Honolulu, Hawaii, 1945.

MacDonald, Gordon Andrew and Hubbard, Douglass H. *Volcanoes of the National Parks in Hawaii.* 3d. Ed. Rev. Hawaii National History Association: Honolulu, Hawai'i, 1965, 1966.

MacDonald, Gordon Andrew and ABBOTT, Agatin T. *Volcanoes in the Sea: The Geology of Hawaii.* University of Hawai'i Press: Honolulu, 1970.

McBride, Leslie R. Pele, *Volcano Goddess of Hawaii.* The Petroglyph Press, Hilo, Hawai'i, 1968.

McBride, Leslie R. *About Hawaii's Volcanoes.* The Petroglyph Press: Hilo, Hawai'i, 1967, 1972.

Mulholland, John Field. *Hawaii's Religions.* Charles E. Tuttle Company, Inc.: Tokyo, Japan, 1970.

Mrantz, Maxine. *Women of Old Hawaii.* Aloha Graphics and Sales: Honolulu, Hawai'i, 1975.

Pukui, Mary Kawena, and Handy, E.S. Craighhill. *The Polynesian Family System in Ka'u, Hawaii.* C. E. Tuttle Co.: Rutland, Vermont, 1972.

Rice, William Hyde. *Hawaiian Legends.* Bernice P. Bishop Museum Bulletin 3, Honolulu, Hawaii, 1923. Kraus Reprint Company: New York, 1971.

Smith, Richard Austin, and Editors of Time-Life Books. *The Frontier States; Alaska, Hawaii.* Time-Life Books: New York, 1970. Copyright 1968, Time Inc.

Westervelt, William Drake. *Hawaiian Legends of Volcanoes.* Charles E. Tuttle Company, Inc.: Rutland, Vermont & Tokyo, Japan, 1963.